In Loving Memory of Reverend Ashley McDonald Buchanan, D.D.

06/19/57 – 12/05/06

My heart is owed by an upright U.S. Citizen Rev. Ashley McDonald Buchanan, D.D., Permanent Teacher. My husband was the most fascinating person I met in 43 years of existence. He was most definitively the best Pastor I found in 22 years with the evangelical churches and I was blessed he accepted to be my husband and I am missing him so much. Not only he was very far from being ignorant like most of them but he was also godly, which is rare these days. This book is dedicated to our ministry he mostly worked on (but the first thing I did when I "studied" Ash is I made sure he was teaching the sound doctrine and more important, that he was applying it) while our governments were keeping us apart from Nov. 3rd, 2004 to June 16th, 2006.

Not only he was a Reverend, he was also an expert/genius of computer science, a poet, a permanent teacher, a photograph and he was about to write a book when he went Home. He also studied psychology (& philosophy) and he got the same conclusion than me (I have a masters degree in psychology) and after all these years of search for the truth – is that the word of the Living God is worth to have our total and complete dedication/consecration and everything else outside God's word and God's will is just dust in the wind.

Heard about The Story of the
Eagle and the Maple Leaf?

For your own sake, you need to hear it.

<u>Here are his own words in my cards:</u>
Postmarked on May 16th, 2005: "On the day they made us part, it tore a hole right through my heart".
Postmarked on February 1st 2006: "all the extra stress these people have caused us has all but killed me".

His words were not only a figure of speech. Ashley is dead now but he is alive in my heart and will always be until my last breath. For the very few folks who know me personally, they know I loved Ash to death.

Song of Solomon 8:

6 Set me as a seal upon thine heart, as a seal upon thine arm: for love is strong as death; jealousy is cruel as the grave: the coals thereof are coals of fire, which hath a most vehement flame.
7 Many waters cannot quench love, neither can the floods drown it: if a man would give all the substance of his house for love, it would utterly be contemned. KJV

Like Ashley said in his poem the Eagle and the Maple Leaf:
They can push and they can shove,
But they cannot kill my love.

The first thing I will do when I will see Ashley again is to tell him a very big thank you for being the wonderful person he was and also I will thank him that I could hang on his words while being away from him....**again**....because his words were true...so I kept everything he told me...Love does not stop nor at the borders, nor at death...it goes beyond the grave!....

Lastly and not the least, I will say a big thank you to my best friend, the Lord Jesus Christ to have made possible not only the Resurrection but also the forgiveness of sins and the power to overcome it while we are on earth in order to avoid the eternal separation from God...The last thing I want is to be eternally separated from the Source of Love, the Source of Life, the Source of Hope, the Truth, the Justice, the Way !!! (Jn. 14:1; Jn. 14:6)

Copyright Notice

ISBN #:	978-0-557-10107-8
Content ID:	7520021
Book Title:	The Story of the Eagle and the Maple Leaf ~ for Love is Strong as Death (Song 8) ~ Rev. Ashley McDonald Buchanan, D.D. Poems

The Eagle and The Maple Leaf

(recorded October 21st, 2005)

One day the cutest Maple leaf,
Found an Eagle filled with grief,
And somehow she touched his soul,
Which made the Eagle feel so whole.

She brought the Eagle so much joy,
He felt just like a little boy.
Now they both felt so much love,
They knew this match was made above.

But now this Eagle rarely sleeps,
Often nights he even weeps,
He cannot see his Maple leaf,
The one that took away the grief.

For the powers made them part,
And this really broke his heart.
And they cannot cross the borders,
This by way of official orders.

They keep from me my precious wife,
The greatest treasure of my life.
They can push and they can shove,
But they cannot kill my love.

Now soon the Eagle which is me,
And my Maple leaf Marie,
Will be together in stronger love,
I give all praise to God above.

Ash

5 Foot 2

Five foot two, with eyes of blue,
Don't you know I love you true?
There's one thing you should know,
Through all this life, with you I go.

Through all the thick and all the thin,
Whether once, or again and again,
There is no one I'd rather see,
On the pillow next to me,

Than the one that married me,
A soft sweet beauty named Marie.
A little secret you must be told,
My love for you will not grow old.

I really wish that I could fly,
For tonight with you I'd lie.
You are so special and so true,
I shall never depart from you.

Ash

A Holy Kiss

A holy kiss just near your lips,
Med hugs above your hips.
There shall nothing spoil our night,
I want it all to be just right.

For you are my greatest treasure,
One for which there is no measure.
You've the sweetest voice I've heard,
And I love your every word.

Now when you become my wife,
You know I'll love you all my life.
And it makes me bend my knee,
To know God brought you to me.

Ash

Angel

As I sit at home tonight feeling all alone,
Suddenly there comes a ring on my telephone.
So I go and answer it to see who it may be,
And I find an Angel who wants to talk to me.

It's a godly woman with a voice that is so sweet,
She's a very special one I know that I must meet.
I've been trying to find her almost all my life,
Now that I have found her, I hope she'll be my wife.

As I sit and talk to her the time just slips away,
For she is so pleasant that the hours melt away.
And the more I know of her, the more I want to know,
Now it's clear that soon I must to this Angel go.

Ash

Another Day

As I end another day,
No good news has come my way.
Now as the sun begins to set,
I haven't seen my dear wife yet.

There is one thing they need to know,
That's I truly love you so.
I long to feel your gentle touch,
I really miss you very much.

I am dying to have you near,
Your whispers in my ear to hear,
When at last we win this fight,
I really want to hold you tight.

We took each other till death do part,
But they insisted from the start.
All throughout the powers that be,
Cold hard hearts is all I see.

Ash

As I Lay Here

As I lay here in my bed,
Heavy heart, as if of lead.
My every thought is of you,
I do not know what to do.

So I sat and sent some notes,
Sailing off like little boats,
Sailing quickly 'cross the seas,
To find people on their knees.

I asked them to go find my friend,
The one I'll love until the end.
I expect to get reactions,
As the words turn into actions.

No mighty winds or storms of hail,
Could ever make this small word fail.
For you see the word is love,
And its power is from above.

Once my words put folks to sleep,
Now they're making people weep.
When you came into my heart,
I knew it was to play some part.

You stirred up such deep emotions,
Deeper than the deepest oceans,
That, love once a tiny word,
Has become a mighty verb.

Ash

Access Denied at The Northern Militarized Borders

MILITARIZATION OF THE NORTHERN BORDERS
http://www.globalresearch.ca/index.php?context=va&aid=14049

Postmark: October 11th, 2004
Ash's reaction letter to the access denied
at the Thousand Island Port of Entry
officially called: Lansdowne POE
on October 9th, 2004

Dear Marie,

I had to write and say I love you again. I can not tell you that I love you often enough. I was so heartbroken when I could not enter Canada to bring you down here. It was not all the driving, the packing or the hours spent at the border that upset me so. It was the fact that I was returning home without the woman I love. (.........) The journey home without the only person on the planet that could ever complete me. It was like leaving a part of my own soul behind in an area where I could not care for it. (.........) I was filled with so much sorrow that I kept crying on the trip home. I pored my heart out to God for hours on end. If there had been even the slightest doubt in my mind as to the depth of my love for you it has been removed. The feelings I have for you are complete and unwavering. There is absolutely nothing in this life or on this planet that I desire more than to be with you. I want to be with you and you only, for the rest of my life. You are the best thing that has ever happened to me and you are truly the greatest blessing I have ever received. To have you as my wife exceeds any blessing that I could have ever conceived of in my own mind. You are truly a gift from God and the greatest treasure I have ever found. I believe anything any greater than you in my life can only come by being in heaven. I love you more than I have ever loved anyone or anything. I cannot imagine anything in my life being better or more desirable than having you by my side. I want you with me always.

With all my love,

Ashley

I will love you always with all that I am. No one shall ever stop me from loving you. You are the only one for me for all time. I cannot wait until we are together. I love you. Ashley

Best Of All

(Recorded April 2nd, 2005)

As I sit here all alone,
It doesn't feel much like home.
I look into my coffee mug,
And realize I miss your hug.

As I sit and count the days,
I realize I miss the ways,
Of soft sweet kisses from your lips,
Your gentle arms around my hips.

There is one thing I'm dying to do,
That is to make sweet love to you.
To hold you in my arms real tight,
To feel you by my side all night.

I know I'll love you till the end,
And you are my very best friend,
I looked for you for all my life,
Now best of all you are my wife.

Ash

Desire

(Recorded October 27th, 2004)

If I could have found a way,
I would have been there yesterday.
For my every living minute,
In my life, I want you in it.

My desire I cannot hide,
I so want you by my side.
You will surely fill my life,
When I have you as my wife.

My very life would I give,
Just to know you as I live.
And my heart sings with glee,
Just to know that you love me.

I surely must be blessed,
You are better than the rest.
All my love shall you know,
For only you will I show.

Ash

Dreams

(Recorded October 27th, 2004)

As I start to fall asleep,
In my head dreams do creep,
And there are no bad dreams there,
They're all of you, a woman fair.

With your smile to light my way,
And happy thoughts of the day,
When we're standing in a place,
With each other face to face.

I know this dream will come true,
When I'm standing next to you.
I would like to hold your hand,
As we walk along the sand.

On the shore of some great ocean,
We may need some suntan lotion.
As we play and have some fun,
Then we'll watch the setting sun.

Now the dream begins to fade,
As the sun peeks 'round my shade,
And the day with light so bright,
Has chased away another night.

Of all the things I dreamed in there,
There wasn't one to compare,
To the beauty of Marie,
She's the only one for me.

Ash

Even Though The End is Near

(Recorded January 18th, 2006)

Even though the end is near,
I still long to have you here,
To be together in this place,
And to see your smiling face.

To hold you in my arms, my dear
And to have you always near,
Is my passion and my drive,
It's what makes me feel alive.

I'm more than ready to start my life,
With you my sweet and loving wife.
On many a long cold winter's night,
I so longed to snuggle tight.

With the one I love so true,
And I know she loves me too.
It's so clear for all to see,
I really love my wife Marie.

Ash

Ever Since

Postmark: January 27th, 2005

Ever since I met you dear
I know that I would want you near
Even though you're not that far
I can't go there in my car

I miss you more than I can say
All night long and every day
When the day comes that we win
We will never part again

All the days feel like years
Most of which are filled with tears
I need the life back in my life
I so need my loving wife

Love,

Ash

Introduction:

This is the first letter
but not our first communication
from the forced separation/partition
at the Militarized Northern Borders.

Dated: Nov. 14th, 2004

Dear Marie,

I love you very very much. I have missed you more than I have ever missed anyone. I love you more than I can express in words and I need to hold you. I cannot believe people could be so cold hearted as to keep us apart. I hope they have already began to reap what they have sown.

To quote God's word is good but it only has meaning to you, me and other believers. God's word means nothing at all to the unbelievers. His word is living and powerful but unfortunately it does not work instantly as we would like. I pray every day for this mess to end and us to be together. I love you so much.

I found a couple of areas to go check out last at (…….). I'll email you if I find something. I talk to you later.

Love,
Ashley

Friend

Date modified: September 23rd, 2004

Here most recent when I had need,
Along came a friend, a friend in deed.
As I rambled through all my fears,
She did listen, with both her ears.

No other person did I find,
To ease the worry in my mind,
All my troubles she put to rest,
Of my friends, she's the best.

Day by day a closer friend,
As she listened without end.
Now one day I hope to see,
My dear friend named Marie.

Ash

Dear Marie,

(Recorded Dec. 9th, 2005)

I thought I would write you this way so you could read it a little more easily this time☺

I really and truly pray that things work out so we can spend this Christmas together, but if they don't I hope it is only a very very short time afterwards.

I have decided to leave all the decorations, stockings and little gifts just as they are until you are here. This way even if it's a little after Christmas before you're here we can still celebrate like you were☺ Tell Mr. Skip and Dashun not to worry – Santa Cat won't take their goodies back if they aren't here at Christmas. Besides, Santa Cat is very easily fooled about dates. Just ask Skip if he knows what the date is☺

I must admit that the idea of spending another Christmas Season alone without you is not a happy thought☹ but every time I think about the fact that I have such a wonderful woman in my life it makes me Praise God and smile ☺☺☺☺☺☺☺☺☺☺ just to know that you will really be here in 3D one day.

I can't wait to open my Christmas Present but something tells me it might be a Little Blue Berry. Did I ever tell you that I just love Blue Berries☺

Here

Recorded Oct. 27th, 2004

As I lay here in my bed,
With dreams of you all through my head,
It is your voice I think I hear,
It makes me think that you are near.

Now as my body tossed and turned,
It was my heart that truly yearned.
To take this vision from my head,
And see you standing here instead.

Ash

Dear Marie,

Recorded September 15th, 2005

I love you more than ever and I miss you
far more than I can Say. So I was thinking
what would I like to say to you this time. The
man in me is mad enough to damage something
over our situation, the husband in me is depressed
and wishes he were there to comfort you, the
Christian in me say "hold on because God is in
control of everything and everything will be fine",
but the little boy in me says: "send her a build a
hippie kit – I bet she doesn't have one".

So, here is your **BUILD A HIPPIE** kit☺
It's really easy to use. Just glue the hair on
The head until you achieve the desired result.
For a Cave-Man look use some hair to connect
The eyebrows, then glue hair everywhere, and
In no time at all you will have your pre-historic
Hippie☺

I hope this brings a smile to your face Sugar☺☺☺

Love, Ash

I DO

Recorded October 27th, 2004
2 days before our marriage

I think it's grand can't you see,
That this woman should love me.
She is a gift from up above,
Wrapped in kindness, filled with love.

In her do my eyes delight,
She's so lovely day or night.
I feel that I must tell her too,
That I love her, this is true.

I so long to have her near,
And two words I want to hear.
For I know she loves me too,
I can't wait to hear I do.

Ash

I Miss You Every Day and Night

I miss you every day and night
I so long to hold you tight
I am so glad you're in my life
I praise God you are my wife

Sent by God from up above
Wrapped in flesh but filled with love
No greater gift could there be
Than to have you here with me

The greatest treasure in my life
Is my dear and precious wife
Now God's love I clearly see
For He's given you to me

With all my love,

Ashley

I Love You So

Recorded October 27th, 2004

I so love you this is true,
For all day long I think of you.
I long for you both day and night,
You are precious in my sight.

Your sweet voice I love to hear,
And I can't wait to have you near.
You are the best thing in my life,
For me you are the perfect wife.

Ash

I Wished Upon a Falling Star

Postmark: January 27th, 2005

I wished upon a falling star
For great wings upon my car
That I could just drive the sky
And across the borders fly

There's one place I want to go
A little town, called Gatineau
In this town I'd like to be
With my wife next to me

I so love her this is true
But the government won't let me through
If I could but fly tonight
I'd go to her and hold her tight

No greater woman could I find
She is truly one of a kind
This special woman called my wife
I shall love for all my life

Ash

January 6th, 2005

Today, Marie and I have decided to start every day by praying together for God's leading. It is now nine weeks and two days since I have seen my wife. I miss Marie more than I have ever missed anyone. I think about her all the time. I still find it hard to believe that the laws of man are of more importance to this world than the will of God. They will reap what they have sown.

January 7th, 2005

Today we heard from a lawyer that Marie wrote over two weeks ago. She seems to have a heart for more than just money. I hope we have judged rightly. On the other side, Marie's hard drive seems to be dying. This is not welcomed news. I had so many things on my mind that I forgot to check (   ) while I was at the library. I know God has heard our prayers and I pray I will be in Canada in the next day or two. We truly cannot take any more heart ache.

January 8th, 2005 Journal

They Broke Our Dreams, Hopes and Lives but Not Our Love

As it has been since Marie and I were separated I got in maybe two or three hours sleep last night.

[Marie's comments:
Ashley before Nov. 3rd, 2004:

Ashley after June 16th, 2006 – the day I Immigrated, I received the Immigrant Visa on June 12th, 2006 – see what does 2-3 hours sleep for 19 months ½, all his hair turned from chestnut to gray. He almost had no gray hair before. Look also how pale is face was.

Yes, he was sick, I am not denying that ~ and I will publish that fact as well and what really happened ~ but fact is that this forced separation did not help his health to the LEAST because I could be far more productive to fight by his side if I would be allowed in the Country. (no criminal records and a masters degree and a various work experience from psychologist and researcher to administrative assistant) As a determined individual as I am, he would have his dialysis and I would give him part of my liver (because our blood was compatible) and he would be alive today. I married him for at least a good 50 years minimum – 50 years would be very quick with this man around me. I would not mind in the least to risk my life for him because he was worth it and in fact I already did by sharing my money with him. (because as you might imagine, the New Word Order began to financially break me on Nov. 3rd, 2004 because back then, I succeed to have a job at the Canadian government, more precisely at the Department of Human Resources and was doing almost 20 dollars an hour – I was not just working through “temp” agencies like most women in the area are doing)

Since we were married, the Ogdensburg border guard and Immigration guard were not supposed to stop me to go back in the US because:

1) we were married;
Even their own laws state this:
It's written this at: http://www.uscis.gov/files/form/I-130instr.pdf,

p. 4. : "When a petition is approved for the husband, wife, parent or unmarried minor child of a United States citizen, these persons are classified as immediate relatives. They do not have to wait for a visa number because immediate relatives are not subject to the immigrant visa limit".

Which means this border guard and this Immigration border agent at Ogdensburg Port of Entry intentionally did not consider their own laws!

2) I had no return date to Canada on my Visa;

3) I even had 90 days to apply for an Immigrant Visa according to the Immigration laws, which was plenty enough to establish my credibility without being parted like vulgar cattle at the borders **for 19 months ½!**

They **DESECRATED** our marriage when God **CONSECRATED** us, which means they now have to deal with God if nobody else will "jump in the plate".

My entry in the US was based on:
1) the US Constitution because Ashley was a US Citizen at least 2 times by being 1) born on the US base, Fort Dix, New Jersey, which made him automatically a US Citizen;
2) served the US Navy, which made him automatically a US Citizen. Read this my dear Americans: US Immigration under the Department of Homeland Security (DHS) went as far as daring to ask Ashley to prove his US Citizenship to try to do everything they could to stop my Immigration process and/or make us wait forever:
See this "crap" for yourself (sorry for the word but even God uses the word "dung" in the bible) – I removed the personal information like the file number:

U.S. Department of Homeland Security
P.O. Box 648006
Lee's Summit, MO 64064

June 28, 2005

ASHLEY BUCHANAN

File #:
A File#:
Form: I-129F

RE: Ashley & Marie Buchanan

Request for Additional Evidence

This office is unable to complete the processing of your Petition for Alien Fiancé, (Form I-129F) without additional information. Please submit the information requested below.

You must submit the information within **87 (eighty-seven)** days **(on or before 09-23-05).** Failure to do so will result in a decision based on the evidence previously submitted. **Please include this letter with your response.** ***Although you may have submitted the requested evidence with other petitions/applications pending with the Service, you must submit the additional evidence requested to continue processing of the I-129F.***

All copies must be clear and legible. Title 8, Code of Federal regulations, 103.2(b) states in part: "(3) **Translations**. Any document containing foreign language submitted to the Service shall be accompanied by a full English language translation which the translator has certified as complete and accurate, and by the translator's certification that he or she is competent to translate from the foreign language into English."

☐ **Please sign and return the attached copy of your I-129 F.**

☐ **3001a Please submit a passport style photo.**
(Photos must have a white or off-white background. Please frame subject with [illegible] front view, eyes open. Photos should present full head from top of hair to bottom of [illegible] height of head should measure 1 inch to 1-3/8 inches (25 mm to 35 mm).

☐ **PETITIONER:** ☐ **BENEFICIARY**

☒ **Please submit evidence that the petitioner Ashley - with /parents' information is a United States Citizen** / A State issued birth certificate *(for immigration purposes, a birth [illegible] provided by the hospital is not consider as proof of U.S. citizenship)*, certificate of naturalization, or a copy of the biographical page of your United States passport.

☐ **Original**	☒ **Copy**	**Birth Certificate**
☐ **Original**	☒ **Copy**	**Passport Biographical Page**
☐ **Original**	☐ **Copy**	**Naturalization Certificate**
☐ **Original**	☐ **Copy**	**Citizenship Certificate**

1

www.uscis.gov

Which means that the US Constitution was not applicable to him anymore (invalidated) because he married an "ALiEn"…what else can I think at this point? They desecrated our marriage and blew up our plans and lives…but that's "ok" it is supposedly to fight "terrorism"...like the Jesuits Maxim, "the end justifies the means", right?...which makes you wonder who the real terrorists are....

If you think they are not actually trying to invalidate the US Constitution right now with this Obama fraudulent administration i.e. our turn is not coming with this Swine Flu Mandatory Vaccine and will kill a lot of US Citizens and Canadians and that's why those plastic crematory coffins as well as the huge crematoriums are for...they are planning to have a lot of people dying and that's why we have industrial quantities of those coffins on US soil... and those Concentration Camps are for the American labor Camp, think again! They are actually hiring your kids....the hottest job out there cracking right now...is internment camp guard, the biggest job the National guard is pushing right now...this has to do with Obama with this sweeping new Federal Police powers...it's all coinciding the mass vaccination drill...it will be mandatory, it will be forced....coming in October this year....hummm, a civilian inmate labor program...how you can get a "civilian inmates"?...inmates are not civilian...civilian means out in the world...they will "herd" you in the camps...to use you for forced labor, don't you think so?...when they begin to hire your kids for internment camp guard, don't you think it's time to wake up????...I am losing my "Latin" right now...

You think the governments did not kill in the human history? Well, you need to check how the governments of this world loved humanity to death throughout history.... The government is the best serial killer ever....You better believe my testimony as a Educated Legal Immigrant from Canada of a Honorably Discharged Vietnam Veteran as this is the truth but most of you won't, I already know that because I am publishing the truth since December 2001 on the internet! **The entire American continent is about to be desecrated...so I ask you to please hear Ash's Wisdom from the grave through his poems....**

The separation was killing him and was killing me as well. Below is the letter to Mrs. Duhanee, who was the right hand or at least the administrative assistant of Minister Monte Solberg, as well as Mr. Solberg Office's reply on his behalf and my last reply to his office. As you will read in the reply of Monte Solberg's office, I was "bothering" all the Members of the Parliament and I even met one of them, namely Marcel Proulx, who was the Member of Parliament of Hull, Quebec, Canada at that time and he said that Ashley was not a criminal and I told him that I was perfectly aware of that and that's exactly why I was fighting so hard to at least have him to be able to visit me in Canada. Yes, Ashley preferred Marie over "Martine" because that would sound "Martin" in the US so I changed for Marie, which is on my birth certificate as well. That's right, I was signing "Martine Hamel" because US Immigration in Ottawa, Canada did not allow me to sign "Marie Buchanan" even if I had my marriage paper with me because they alleged that all my ID's were under "Martine Hamel" but my marriage paper was superceding all my ID's according to the laws of the land and they told me the Immigration process would end there if I would not sign: "Martine Hamel". Needless to say that we already were in a big mess created by the Northern

Militarized Borders (US side: Ogdensburg Port of Entry and Canadian side: Officer Mona Scott, Prescott Port of Entry) and it would be a big deal to do my change of name in Canada by changing all my ID's, including my social security number and all my energy was invested in the fight to see Ashley's face a.s.a.p. since the separation on Nov. 3rd, 2004 so don't throw stones at me for not changing my name because the ones you need to throw stones at is DHS. All my official papers in Canada were under "Martine Hamel" and all my official papers in US are under "Marie M. Buchanan" since the day 1 I finally put my feet on the US soil **again**, i.e. June 16th, 2006, which means I immigrated the same week I finally received my Immigrant Visa on June 12th, 2006.

March, 22th, 2006

Dear Mrs. Duhanee,

Thank you for your kind advice and assistance.

I am a Canadian citizen, that married an American, Ashley McDonald Buchanan. We where married on October 29th, 2004, in Union County, North Carolina.

My husband and I attempted entry into Canada on Noverber 3rd, 2004, via the Prescott Port of entry. (POE) Unfortunately, my husband has had 2 previous DWI convictions in the U.S. Incidents dating back to a time when he was faced with great personal tragedy. Both incidents date back to 1979 and 1996.

Because of this, I decided to immigrate to the U.S. myself but as you know, the process can take some time. This process also prevents me from visiting my husband, in the U.S.

I have been writing for so long to so many people. I am so very discouraged by this situation.

All I would ask, is that my husband be allowed to visit me. I don't have much money. I can not afford a lawyer. You are my last hope in Canada, Minister Solberg.

I do hope to hear from you very soon.

With Kind Regards,

Martine Hamel, M.Ps.

Email addresses: marie4ashley@copper.net, marielovesashley@yahoo.ca, mariemartine1966@yahoo.com

c.c. The Honourable Stephen Harper

Hamel, Martine

From: CIC - Ministerial Enquiries Division/CIC - Service de renseignements ministériels [Ministerial.Enquiries.Division@cic.gc.ca]

Sent: Wednesday, March 22, 2006 3:48 PM

To: Hamel, Martine

Cc: marie4ashley@copper.net; mariemartine1966@yahoo.com; marie4martine@aol.com

Subject: Overcoming Criminal Inadmissibility

Dear Martine Hamel:

I am replying to your various correspondence addressed to several members of Parliament as well as the Minister of Citizenship and Immigration, concerning the immigration situation of your husband, Ashley Buchanan.

Unfortunately, there is very little that I can add to what has already been repeatedly conveyed to you and your husband by officials of Citizenship and Immigration Canada. Persons who have been convicted of most criminal offences are inadmissible to Canada, according to Canadian immigration legislation. For example, while we understand that some persons do not consider impaired driving as a crime, its presence in the Canadian Criminal Code is recognition of the serious consequences of this offence.

When an inadmissible person seeks entry at a Canada at a port of entry, the examining officer has three options:

- To allow the person to withdraw voluntarily;
- To refuse the person admission and make him or her the subject of a formal report under the *Immigration and Refugee Protection Act*; or,
- To allow the person to enter on a Temporary Resident Permit (TRP).

While an individual may have been admitted as a visitor in the past, it does not guarantee that permission to enter Canada will be given in the future.

An inadmissible person can also seek permanent removal of the inadmissibility BEFORE arriving in Canada, by way of an Application for rehabilitation. Rehabilitation means the persons can show that they have a stable lifestyle and it is unlikely that they will be involved in any further criminal activity. For persons convicted outside Canada, the granting of relief from the inadmissibility may be approved by a Canadian Visa office abroad, provided that five years have passed since the commission of the offence, along with any sentence imposed. If less than five years have elapsed, or if the persons are only seeking entry to Canada for a temporary period, then they may qualify for a TRP. Persons who are ineligible for approval of rehabilitation because not enough time has passed should complete the forms and check "For Information Only." An officer will decide if a TRP is warranted. Please contact the nearest Canadian Visa office for additional information or to submit an application.

While I realize that this is not the reply you had anticipated, I hope you will find this information useful.

This electronic address is not available for response.

March, 22th, 2006

Dear Mrs. Duhanee,

In response to your most recent email, please consider the following:
Immigration and refugee Protection act, Vol. 138, No. 16 – August 11th, 2004.
Paragraph 36 (2) (B):

(**b**) persons convicted outside Canada of two or more offences that, if committed in Canada, would constitute summary conviction offences under any Act of Parliament, if all of the following conditions apply, namely,

(i) at least **five years** have elapsed since the day after the completion of the imposed sentences,

(ii) the person has not been convicted in Canada of an indictable offence under an Act of Parliament,

(iii) the person has not within the **last five years** been convicted in Canada of an offence under an Act of Parliament, other than an offence designated as a contravention under the Contraventions Act or an offence under the Youth Criminal Justice Act,

(iv) the person has not within **the last five years** been convicted outside Canada of an offence that, if committed in Canada, would constitute an offence under an Act of Parliament, other than an offence designated as a contravention under the Contraventions Act or an offence under the Youth Criminal Justice Act,

(v) the person has not before **the last five years** been convicted in Canada of more than one summary conviction offence under an Act of Parliament, other than an offence designated as a contravention under the Contraventions Act or an offence under the Youth Criminal Justice Act,

Published at:
http://canadagazette.gc.ca/partII/2004/20040811/html/sor167-e.html

We fully understand the scope and spirit of the Law. We do not contest the Law. The Law was not applied as it is read. More than five (5) years have elapsed since any of the incidents. Therefore, on what ground was my husband refused entry into Canada? Please explain this to me.

Thank you for your very kind attention.

Martine Hamel

Martine Hamel, M.Ps.

Email addresses: marie4ashley@copper.net, marielovesashley@yahoo.ca, mariemartine1966@yahoo.com

c.c. The Honourable Stephen Harper

My last employer, Statistics Canada, wanted me to give 2 weeks notice…well, US Immigration were not giving me a cue of when I would receive it so you think I would wait another 2 weeks to not waste money in Canada after those 19 months ½ of precious time with Ash wasted? All I wanted is to be in the presence of my Charming Scottish Prince***. Also, my landlord wanted me to pay the month of July 2004 when in fact I was leaving on June 16th, 2004 and the month was paid until June 30th. Of course, I could not give them a notice to any of them because when you deal with DHS, (US Immigration is under Department of Homeland Security) you are dealing with the unexpected, that's a proven fact….Jean-Pierre was mean with me and was continuously telling me that I did not have a husband (Ash called him one time and he told my husband there was no "Martine Hamel" there but Ashley knew I was there not only because he had the whole name of the landlord and his private phone number…but also Ashley knew me very well…) and now he was crying to not get extra money for the month of July (they made me cry a couple of times) and his wife was hitting hard the widow of the U-Haul truck because she felt to beat me up…For the very few folks who know me, they know if I could give a notice to my employer as well as my landlord, I would….yes, there was a hole in the wall because I was not only tired to have Jean-Pierre telling me that I did not have a husband but also US Immigration did return me back in Canada for our Christmas season present in 2004 (one month after the forced separation) …this was at the Roosevelt Port of Entry…I was saying that I was visiting my best friend…I knew what would happen if I would say that I was visiting my husband but Ashley was my best friend as well…they were about ten (10) on my case and I was about to enter when one of them shouted: "I saw your face on t.v. You are married! You will not enter!" So here is the "wonderful" paperwork to prove this happened:

U.S. IMMIGRATION 001

U.S. Department of Justice
Immigration and Naturalization Service

Applicant for Admission Advisement

Date of Inspection: 12/04/2004
Time of Inspection: 7 10 pm

MS Marie Bastine Hamed

Dear Applicant for Admission:

At this time, you do not appear to be clearly admissible to the United States as a temporary visitor for pleasure. In order to satisfy Immigration Officials as to your status and intentions, please provide this office with the items checked below.

This list is intended to be used as a guideline to assist you in returning with the necessary materials to sufficiently meet the burden of proof incumbent upon you as an applicant for admission to the United States. **This list should not be considered to be all inclusive and it is not a guarantee of admission to the United States. The final decision of admission is always made by an Immigration Inspector after all items/facts are considered.**

- [x] **Evidence of Citizenship**
- [ ] **Evidence of Employment**
  ie: recent pay stubs, employment ID, letter of employment, etc.
- [x] **Evidence of Foreign Residence**
  ie: various utility bills- recent phone, gas, electric, water, recent rent receipts, copy of mortgage, deed, etc
  Agreement between You and Lessor
- [x] **Evidence of Financial Ability**
  ie: bank statements, savings and checking account transaction books, income tax forms, etc.
- [x] **Evidence of Financial Assistance**
  ie: unemployment insurance, welfare, disability, in the form of current stubs, receipts, government correspondence.
- [ ] **Evidence of Educational Ties**
  ie: valid school ID, letter from school official, current course registration, etc.
- [x] **Evidence of confirmed means of departure from the United States**
  ie: plane, train, bus, etc (date specific; non-refundable)
- [x] **Evidence of Sufficient Funds for Intended Length of Stay**
  ie: cash, travellers checks, personal checks, credit cards, etc.
- [x] **Evidence of Contact Person**
  ie: family member, friend, or individual whom you are travelling to see in the United States.
- [x] **Address/Telephone Number Where You Can be Reached in the United States**
  ie: recent pay stubs, employment ID, Letter of employment, etc
- [ ] **Other:**

See CBPEO Suffokta Monday 12/05/2004 through Friday 12/10/2004 9am-5pm

Phone
(315) 764 0677
(315) 764-0310

Ashley told me they were asking as much as the petition for fiancée or the Immigrant Visa and told me I should not try again and wait....He called Mr. Suffokta and Mr. Suffokta told him that even if I would provide everything mentioned on the paper, that was not a guarantee as the papers states above....I would enter and the price of going at the borders by bus was the same as a taxi cab...I did not have a car, otherwise, I would try....and nobody to care for me in Canada so I took the taxi cab...

....because Ashley got "this John Friot" to interview him at his hotel room and to interview me on the phone and put my picture on t.v. Ashley and I were hoping it would go farther than that but our efforts were aborted right there....and turned against us instead. I asked many times to the News Director Scott Atkinson of Fox WWNY to give me my video and I have all the reasons to believe something is fishy here....I am requesting it since April 1st, 2007...on July 11th, 2007, he told me to give him a couple of days...this is at least two (2) years after...and told me to take a deep breath on January 26th, 2008...**I have all the life to wait, right?** So now the emails are going in my book:

About Scott Atkinson, News Director WWNY

this video was the irrefutable proof that we did not want this separation and that they separated us at the Militarized Northern Border....precisely, it was the irrefutable proof that the border agent as well as the US Immigration agent at the Ogdensburg Port of Entry really did a big mess according to the US Constitution........waiting for the video to come yet....

and I could not bear it anymore, I did this hole with my feet ...but Jean-Pierre was working in the construction so it was not a big deal to take care of that hole...a human can take as much dung as they can but eventually, it turns the meekest person into somebody who eventually makes holes in the walls...because she was "over-broke" inside...that was too much heart ache, over heart ache...I almost hear those Christian evangelicals under Rome saying: "bad, bad, girl"...I am a meek person yet, Thank God for that because He is the one who kept me safe and sound but I am not a "defenseless" victim anymore, over my dead body....I am almost sure Therese still hates me for not paying the month of July 2004 nor for not being able to give a month notice like our verbal agreement stipulated it but they broke me financially at the borders and I could not give a month notice nor 2 weeks but who cares? God does care...

If I will join Ashley in Heaven soon, (I dreamed last night which means September 3rd I was joining him in another State, that was such a sweet dream, I did not want it to end....) I want this to be published as a testimony against the Militarized Northern Borders for all those genuine couples out there who really and truly love each other and are passing through this "crap" as well as all those families parted at the borders because I am fully aware that a lot of Americans have family members in Canada and a lot of Canadians have family members in the US. After all, 9 Provinces on 10 are English speaking people...

Here is the letter of support of my friend Adam Bartlett wrote around March 26th, 2007

ADB4JESUS@aol.com wrote:
Marie,
I have attached my letter for you, send it to who ever is needed and make copies and send it to as many people as you think will help in this situation. God bless,
Adam

Alpha & Omega

Outreach Ministries

P.O.Box 34 Boonville, Indiana 47601

Adam Bartlett: Cell:, email: adb4jesus@aol.com

Kevin Wilson: Cell:, email: kjw1975

Web Page: www.bibleheadquarters.org

To Whom It May Concern:

I have known Marie Buchanan for about 6-7 years and I also knew of her marriage to Mr. Ashley Buchanan. I also know of the ministry they shared and have participated in it with them on several occasions. I have followed Marie's battle with the American Government since her marriage and trying to get into the United States and gain citizenship. It is amazing to me how many "illegals" get the red carpet treatment yet a Veteran and his new bride are treated like communists.

The ordeal that Marie has had to endure throughout her marriage and Ashley's illness and subsequent death is something you would expect in a communist country. I am appalled at the way this situation has been handled and most especially the treatment in making Marie's transition into our country and literal nightmare.

I believe there should be a complete investigation into the V.A. Hospital that treated Ashley and I believe criminal charges should be filed against those that were negligent. As for the current situation about Marie's status into this country, that should not even be in question. This government owes it to the wife of a Veteran to make this situation right and stop harassing her in her attempt to become a citizen.

With treatment like this it is no surprise that there are hundreds of thousands of "illegals" because trying to do what is right is impossible with our incompetent government.

As an American citizen and a Veteran of our Armed Forces I am imploring you to do the right thing and stop this crazy charade with Marie.

Sincerely, Adam Bartlett

Marie

Friday, August 14, 2009 5:20 PM
From: "recticuli"
The Liberty Silver Nugget
To:
mariemartine1966@yahoo.com
All together I have know Marie Buchanan now for a little over 2 years. Through the net and personally. everything she has told you has been the truth. She is not lying about her physical condition in the least.

Not only did the government drag her and Ashley through the mud over the immigration thing, which should never have happened, if immigration had only adhered to the guidelines that had been set by CONGRESS, and at their own site....not to mention the VA and their medical mistreatment of Ashley, the VA could have save Ashley by allowing Dialysis Treatment. Then to top it off, Ashley and Marie had no money set aside for his burial... She had no idea of the burial benefits Ashley was entitled to either.

She was so stressed out I am surprised that she didn't have a heart attack the night I walk around with her.... to get her calmed down..

She does have physical problems other than stress as well. she was not able to eat right... she buries herself into her work, which can be bad at times, because she doesn't break off enough to give her mind and body the needed nourishment and rest. Her station was 15 feet from mine.... so I did get to know her quite well...

She never once came onto me.... which I was happy about... because I have no designs of getting involved with any females or anyone else...

As for Eric Jon Phelps lies, Phelps tried to paint a rosy picture of himself, which was easy to see through.

Marie's comments but I do agree with my friend above: To bury myself in work is my way to survive/stay alive in this New World DISoRdEr and this so wonderful world…everybody and everyone stripped me off of all I had as much as they could …I almost lost hope in humanity on the American continent at this point….

….here's how much money I got for the house (the house of Ashley's father) and I had to sign it because I had no money left in my bank account (not because I was dumb) because I could not work because I did not have my green card, except this low fixed income which is the widow pension. All widows of US Veterans know how much I am receiving per month. That's my copy and I forgot to take another copy with the date on it but I do have in my archives the US Post office tracking number and the date on it. By the way, there was no dispute simply because I needed money so bad, I was stuck in the State of GA and I wanted to come back to where Ash is buried, which is my home. It's or in Anne Buchanan Green or their mind but it was not on mine. The dispute was between Stephen Buchanan, Ash's son and Anne Buchanan Green, Ash's sister.

SETTLEMENT AGREEMENT AND RELEASE

THIS SETTLEMENT AGREEMENT ("Agreement") is made as of this _____ day of __________, 2008 by and among ANNE BUCHANAN GREEN and MARIE BUCHANAN

RECITALS

WHEREAS, Anne Buchanan Green and Marie Buchanan are heirs to Herald Dean Buchanan;

WHEREAS, a dispute has arisen between the parties regarding their respective interests in the real estate of Herald Dean Buchanan;

WHEREAS, pursuant to the terms and conditions of this Agreement, the Parties desire to fully, finally, and forever settle and resolve all disputed matters among them and release each other from any further payments, obligations and liabilities;

NOW, THEREFORE, for good and valuable consideration, including the promises and mutual covenants herein contained, the receipt and sufficiency of which is hereby acknowledged, the Parties hereby agree as follows:

AGREEMENT

1. **Payment**

In consideration of the release and discharge and the mutual promises set forth herein, Anne Buchanan Green shall pay Marie Buchanan the sum of Three Thousand Six Hundred and Seventy-Seven Dollars ($3,677.00) This sum shall be paid out of the funds Anne Buchanan Green receives at the sale of the property located at 5209 Reid Road, Indian Trail, North Carolina ("Reid Road Property"). T~~he closing for the Reid Road Property is scheduled for June 2, 2008~~.

2. **Release and Discharge**

Upon receipt of the payment described in paragraph 1, Marie Buchanan shall release any claim that he has or may have to any proceeds of the sale of the Reid Road Property or to the estate of Herald Dean Buchanan.

Except as to any claim based upon a breach of this Agreement, the Parties, in consideration of the payment described in Paragraph 1 above and for other valuable consideration, shall completely release and forever discharge each other from any and all claims, demands, causes of action, damages and costs of any kind or nature from the beginning of time through the execution of this Agreement. This release on the part of Parties shall be a fully binding and complete settlement between the Parties, and shall represent and inure to the benefits

Here is the supposedly Last Will and Testament of Herald Dean Buchanan:

Last Will and Testament of Herald Dean Buchanan

I, Herald Dean Buchanan, being of sound mind and capable for making important decisions, do this seventh day of May, 2005 will all of my worldly possession to my only daughter, Anne Elizabeth Buchanan Green. This is inclusive of the home where I presently reside at 5209 Reid Road, Indian Trail, North Carolina and all the land where the house is situated and the remainder listed in legal documents at the Union County Court House, Monroe, North Carolina. Also this is to give my daughter, Anne Buchanan Green legal authority to pay all outstand bills, unpaid taxes, as well as access to all my banking accounts with the absolute freedom to exercise her own prerogative as for all final decisions concerning my material properties.

As for my only son, he has already received his fair share of my worldly possession during my lifetime. Therefore, this will makes no claim as for leaving my son, Ashley MacDonald Buchanan anything more than what he received from me during my lifetime. He will understand this statement at the reading of this will following the burial of my remains.

This is to request that my remains be transferred to Fox and Weeks Funeral Home in Savannah, Georgia. After a brief funeral conduced in keeping with my requests submitted to my daughter, Anne Buchanan Green while I am alive and still possess necessary mental faculties necessary for supporting this appeal. After a few brief words by my daughter's choice of a Baptist minister and reading Bible scripture, both to transpire at a graveside service, the only music to be that from my eldest grandson, Christopher Scott Green playing on the last trumpet I gave to him, one stanza of "Jesu, Joy of Man's Desiring."

All preceding wills and statements dealing with my death and earthly remains are herby null, void, and hereby superseded, being replaced by this document, dated this seventh day of May, 2005.

Herald D. Bu[illegible]

Herald Dean Buchanan

Witnessed by:

STATE OF NORTH CAROLINA
COUNTY OF UNION

SUBSCRIBED, SWORN TO AND ACKNOWLEDGED BEFORE ME BY HERALD DEAN BUCHANAN, THE TESTATOR, PERSONALLY KNOWN TO ME THIS 7TH DAY OF MAY, 2005.

Michael L. Louviere, NOTARY PUBLIC

(OFFICIAL SEAL)

MICHAEL L. LOUVIERE
NOTARY PUBLIC
MECKLENBURG COUNTY, N.C.
My Commission Expires 9-26-2006

Here is Ashley's Renunciation of this document – yes, his words were the truth and I am "allowing him" to speak on that issue because his sister was not that good towards him:

March 3, 2006

Re: Estate of Herald Dean Buchanan

Dear Mr. Sitton:

1. In regard to the Renunciation you mailed to me I will not sign it. My sister, Anne B. Green will just have to trust me, as I have had to trust her in watching over my personal possessions there in North Carolina.
2. To ask that I sign such a document exhibits a lack of trust on her behalf, although I have never given her any reason to not trust me.
3. The zeal with which I was presented with this Affidavit and its eagerly anticipated execution lead me to question the motivation behind it.
4. This has in turn caused me to examine the copy of the Will you furnished.

    A. My first observation is that the Will contains misspellings, which is unusual for a man that spent his life teaching Secondary English, preparing students for the S.A.T. and had been writing a book over the past several years.
    B. After forty-eight years my father forgot how to spell my name even though I am named after his favorite brother, my grandfather and spent ten of the last eleven years of his life living him and taking care of him? Yet the spelling of my sister's name is perfect.
    C. My father's funeral requests were never submitted to my sister. Anne called me trying to find the name of the funeral home in Savannah, Georgia that handled our mother's funeral.
    D. Why would my father ask Anne to select a Baptist preacher and Scripture to be read when I am a Seminary Graduate and Ordained Baptist Minister?
    E. Why does the Notary Statement at the bottom of the Will look like it was written by a small child?

F. My father personally appeared before a Notary in Union County, NC that happens to be commissioned in Mecklenburg County, NC?

G. My father's signature on the Will has variations which are not present in any of the samples I have of his handwritings or signatures spanning decades and as current as Christmas of 2005. This was determined through computer analysis and overlays of the samples.

5. In conclusion I can only say that my father, Herald Dean Buchanan, was not the author of this will. As I stated in the beginning: My sister, Anne B. Green will just have to trust me as I have had to trust her in watching over my personal possessions there in North Carolina. She needs to learn that she can believe my words without a sworn written oath.

Matt 5:37 But let your communication be, Yea, yea; Nay, nay: for whatsoever is more than these cometh of evil. (KJV)

Sincerely,

Rev. A. M. Buchanan, D.D.

Anne is the typical American woman – she is after $$$. Yes, I am exposing her because she is another one who harmed me. Read first before judging me. She even removed from the original amount 5000 $ for the house:

1) what her own late husband gave to me from his pockets after Ashley's death - 500$; (he was not lending me this money)

2) and to reimburse her the 500$ she "gave" me at my husband's funerals as well as;

3) to ask me to reimburse the 323$ she spent to send Ash's books to "Mac" (that's the way she was calling him, from McDonald and Ash hated "Mac") by arguing that my husband told he would reimburse her but I could not do otherwise because she removed the money from the little check I was about to receive with her attorney's help.

The power is to those who have money, right? The justice and the truth is the last thing we find in those Masonic institutions and professions, it's a proven fact....

....so she deducted 1323 $ from the little initial 5000 $. (folks, this deal was made last year (July 2008) so don't enter in contact with me in hope to get the few money I had from that house, it's gone. Well, better to be safe than sorry those days....)

And she is, to top all of it off, supposed to be my co-sponsor because I am what is called those days a "legal Immigrant". Yes, after all those 18 months of waiting this Immigration process to be over, they first denied my Immigrant Visa on May 24th, 2006 because they covertly said (not overtly) that "Ash was too poor to have a wife". **To be in the presence of the most beautiful gift God has ever put into my life, My Charming Scottish Prince, I was denied even the shortest glimpse after all those horrible 18 months was literally unbearable.**

THE FOREIGN SERVICE
OF THE
UNITED STATES OF AMERICA

Date 24-May-2006
Visa Symbol CR1

HAMEL, Marie Martine
(LAST NAME, First, Middle)

Dear Visa Applicant,

This office regrets to inform you that it is unable to issue a visa to you because you have been found ineligible to receive a visa under the following section(s) of the Immigration and Nationality Act. The information contained in the paragraphs marked with "X" pertain to your visa application. Please disregard the unmarked paragraphs.

[X] Section 221(g) which prohibits the issuance of a visa to anyone whose application does not comply with the provisions of the Immigration and Nationality Act or regulations issued pursuant thereto. The following remarks apply in your case:*

Please obtain the following:

A joint sponsor, or please show enough income to meet the requirements of the I-864 form. It requires a single sponsor to have income of $16,500. If your income is below this level, please find a joint sponsor. The joint sponsor must be a U.S. citizen or Lawful Permanent Resident who is domiciled in the U.S. The joint sponsor must also execute an original Form I-864 Affidavit of Support and provide copies of his U.S. federal income tax returns for the last three tax years. Form I-864 is available online at www.uscis.gov

[ ] Section 212(a)(1) health-related grounds.

[ ] Section 212(a)(4) which prohibits the issuance of a visa to anyone likely to become a public charge.

[ ] Section 212(a)( )( )

See Form DSL-851A for further details.

[ ] Other:

[X] Further consideration will be given to your visa application after you obtain and present the documents listed above and/or the following:*

[ ] You are eligible for waiver of the grounds of ineligibility. To apply for a waiver, follow the instructions on the attached Form I-724.

*WARNING: IF YOU FAIL TO TAKE THE ACTION REQUESTED WITHIN ONE YEAR FOLLOWING VISA DENIAL UNDER SECTION 221(G) OF THE IMMIGRATION AND NATIONALITY ACT, SECTION 223(G) OF THE ACT REQUIRES THAT YOUR APPLICATION BE CANCELLED.

Sincerely yours,

American Consular Officer

NSN 7540-00-149-0995
50194-104

PREVIOUS EDITIONS USABLE

OPTIONAL FORM 194 (Rev. 4-91)
U.S. DEPARTMENT OF STATE

So she could at the very least be fair with me concerning the 500 $ her late husband gave to me…because he was dead, he could not voice his opinion anymore….if nothing else…well, in fact she did not even respected her own late husband, he gave this money to me….now, do you understand why I say that she is the typical American woman? (men know what it means)

Like this would not be enough and to crown the whole thing, the border guard at Fort Covington Port of Entry almost prevented me to bury my own husband on December 12th, 2006. That's right, I was harassed and it is by the skin of the teeth that I remained in the Country…the only thing that prevented the **ultimate**

desecration (not be able to bury my own husband) to happen is that I mentioned Congressman John M. McHugh knows my case since December 2005…

Without forgetting the fact that Ashley's furniture (my furniture and books) were stolen in Herald Dean Buchanan's garage (somebody broke in the garage door) and Ashley was trusting his sister Anne to watch over his personal possessions in North Carolina like he said in his letter re: Estate of Herald Dean Buchanan above….it's not because he was dead, this trust could be trashed…she did not watch over…right after Stephen Buchanan (Ashley's "biological" son, he is not acting like his father to the least so that's why I do not recognize him as Ash's son even if he is, he is for me Ellen's son….Ellen was Ashley's first wife…and it will stay that way until he will really change his attitudes and behavior…) saw he could not get a couple of things I had left when he came at his father's funerals. Anne allegedly reported to the police the incident but said Stephen did it and alleged she did not want to tell that to the police to save Stephen few problems because he is already known by the police in North Carolina. On the other side, Stephen alleged it is Anne who took the furniture and books. I will not split the hair in four here, the "family" stole my things (whether it is Anne or Stephen, I'll let them to dispute between themselves [like they did for the house] the title and crown of "Who is The Most eViL" between this Satanist ~ according to late Johnny Mercer Green ~ and this evangelical Christian) when I was stuck in GA with no money in my bank account.

I kept all my papers but I did not want to put you to sleep with my story… Just to give you a glimpse, a "taste" of what happened to allow you to appreciate the poems more…. I could write a thick book about all that happened to me since Nov. 3rd, 2004….

Back to Ashley's journal entry: When I left the hotel today it was snowing pretty hard. It was not very cold I guess because there was little to no wind. Today overcast with low visibility made it hard to see very far. The sky was as white as the ground. The roads were not very slick so driving was no problem. We waited all day for the lawyer to call but he never did. There was no new email either. So another day goes by without each other. How can people be so cruel as to separate newlyweds and not care.

LIFE

What is this thing we call time?
A measure for this life of mine?
A lifetime is but a puff of smoke,
In eternity, just a joke.

We are here but for a season,
We all try to find a reason,
We all want a life worth living,
We all have love for giving.

A desire for someone there,
When it's time our love to share.
Someone to call on the phone,
Someone there when we are home.

One to entrust your greatest secret,
Knowing that they'll surely keep it.
As a man and for my life,
This would surely be my wife.

And her beauty stops not with skin,
For it comes from deep within,
Welling up from her soul,
For The Lord has made her whole.

Nothing shall ever, our love sever,
For it's God who joins together.
We'll be together until the end,
She is my wife, my lover, and friend.

Ash

MAIN ISSUES WITH THE VA OFFICE OF MASSENA, NY

June 16th, 2008

My husband suffocated twice while waiting for a bed available in Syracuse – I had to meet the team (the nurse and the social worker) and tell them to not wait for a bed in Syracuse but to work on getting a bed a.s.a.p. to another VA hospital because it was taking forever.

The diagnostic of the hepatitis "C" was known by my husband about just 2 months before his death and we do know how hepatitis "C" is destroying a liver and I may got it because of the real incompetence of the VA Office in Massena established July 19th, 2006 but Ashley really tried to get help before that date and all they were offering is to fill a form to ask for benefits and my husband told them he was already receiving benefits – he was not heard and that is why he began to be officially established at this specific date. I am almost sure nobody prescribed steroids or antiviral drugs to reduce the liver cell injury because my husband never mentioned that to me and he was mentioning everything to me. If I would know he had hepatitis "C" I would tell him to call the Georgetown University Hospital and be on the liver transplant list with a living donor which would be me because our blood was at least compatible if not the same type (A+) and it is far quicker if you have your living donor with you than to wait for a cadaver and Ashley could even get the Immigration process to be over quicker for me because his living donor was in Canada dying to join him and his case was the most urgent.

MAIN ISSUES WITH THE ALBANY VA MEDICAL CENTER
FROM OCT 19TH TO NOV. 22TH, 2006

June 16th, 2008

Only at the very end of the hospitalization they were considering to put my husband on a liver transplant list (when in fact, it takes many, many months to go on the top of it) which is the most ridiculous idea considering the state he was when he entered there on Oct. 19th, 2006 by ambulance from Massena Memorial Hospital. That should be the first thing considered and evaluated urgently, not at the very last minute because of the time consuming business of going to the top of this list.

Why do you think Ashley did not want to have the evaluation of what was inside his liver was cancer or not at the very last minute? (you in general, not you in particular) Because from Oct. 19th, to Nov. 22th, 2006, he was very mistreated/received bad services and he had more than enough. All this time of waiting was only and just to remove the liquid inside his lungs and get a simple procedure called tips to be done and this could have been a done deal in two weeks. As an example, he got his surgery without any painkiller – even the doctor Ming Fey Luo told me this. This is so true that when he finally entered at the Massena Memorial Hospital where he finally died, he refused to be transferred to a VA hospital and no matter which one simply because they totally made him sick of them all because he was never heard as a patient.

Too much proteins in his diet for somebody who was having a liver problem (I am a researcher and I did my own search) and they changed his diet at the very last minute but it was too late because he developed problems he never had before at home with his liver – I mean never. His liver got worse and this is so true that he became yellow only 4 days after his hospital release but we were both so very scared he would be transferred again at a VA hospital that I tried my very best to solve the problem at home (because I wanted to respect my husband's wishes to not be back to a hospital, not even the one at Massena) but I had to realize it was not just a matter of having too much ammonia going straight to his brain because of his liver not functioning properly and that is why I called the ambulance even if my husband did not want to go to the hospital again. So since it was over my competence I capitulated and I called the ambulance, believing I was making the best decision for Ashley because I thought they would do everything they could to save my husband's life.

My Dear Marie

Recorded: October 27th, 2004
2 days before our marriage

There is a woman I hold dear,
A special one that I want near,
To her I give a holy kiss,
She's the one I do miss.

A special treasure filled with love,
I know she's sent from above.
For her I've looked for all my life,
And now she said she'd be my wife.

Let me not forget to mention,
She has captured my attention,
It is very plain to see,
This special woman's named Marie.

Ash

Me and You

Recorded May 17th, 2005

Even though you're far away and we are still apart,
Every time I look inside I find you in my heart.
Each and every thought of you so makes me feel alive,
The very thought of holding you gives my life its drive.

I don't want to make a plan that does not include you,
For I want you to be part of everything I do.
Yes there are, still some things, that we need to work out,
And about each other, we're still finding out.

All about those little things that help to form a bond,
For a strong relationship that lasts for years beyond.
I've grown tired of single life, which yields excessive strife,
I would so much, rather say, this woman is my life.

So anything you want to do, we will find a way,
For I want you happy, each and every day.
I think you're really special, yes these words are true,
Once we have, worked all out, then it's me and you.

Love,

Ashley

My Dear Marie

Recorded September 19th, 2004

Any time I'm feeling blue,
All I need is think of you,
All my troubles melt away,
And it is a brighter day.

Enchanting visions all so true,
Are the ones I have of you,
I so hope to see the day,
When I find you've come to stay.

If cold outside you know we'll huddle,
If inside we're sure to cuddle,
I wish each morn to wake and see,
That you're lying next to me.

Any time we're not together,
Regardless of the type of weather,
There's one thing you know I'll miss,
It's the taste of your sweet kiss.

And a thought I hold dear,
Is the one of you so near,
Be you dressed in jeans or lace,
I long to give you an embrace.

To gently wrap my arms around you,
And to say I'm glad I found you.
Another like you they'll never be,
And you mean so much to me.

Ash

My Life

Recorded: October 27th, 2004
2 days before our Marriage on October 29th, 2004

There was a time back in the past,
I did not want my life to last.
Filled with loneliness and despair,
There was no happiness found in there.

My heart was broken right in two,
For in my life there was not you.
I had no one to share my life,
There was no woman as my wife.

I felt my life was less than dust,
I had no treasure only rust.
Now there was no joy I had,
For all my days were only sad.

I asked my God to help me please,
I begged of Him down on my knees.
To fill my life with love that's true,
Then He went and sent me you.

We were friends right from the start,
Soon I found you in my heart.
In my life I trust you to stay,
I love you more each passing day.

Ash

My Mind

Recorded: July 13th, 2005

If you climb into my mind,
I'll tell you what you'll find.
Some folks might find this odd,
But I'm talking to my God.

I have to thank Him this you see,
For He's given you to me.
Him I love and Him I praise,
He gave me you for all my days.

In your eyes I see the love,
Of my Creator from above.
A special woman, no mistake,
A beauty only God could make.

If I were Adam you'd be my Eve.
For all my life to you I'll cleave.
You are the best thing in my life,
And I'm blessed you are my wife.

With all my love,

Ashley

My Wife Marie

Recorded: August 17th, 2005

What is the value of my wife?
She's worth more than my life,
More than the total of her parts,
The greatest, which is her heart.

She truly has a heart of gold,
I know I'll love her when I'm old.
I love her more with every breath,
I'm sure to love her till my death.

She is a sweet and special treasure,
She brings my life unmeasured pleasure,
It isn't how she combs her hair,
And it isn't just her skin so fair.

It's the way she loves me true,
And I know she loves God too.
Her beauty is much more than skin,
For it comes from deep within.

Ash

Nimesh Desai at the left and James Burnett at the right

Nimesh Desai decided to **NOT** even **OFFER** a dialysis to my late husband I called the Congressman McHugh on Dec. 1st 2006 to explain they where letting my husband shut down and the office of the Congressman McHugh called the Hospital Officials on Dec. 2nd. 2006 so Ash and I were having hope but this was in vain because Mr. Desai (who was the "doctor" responsible for Ashley's care) did not change his "course" i.e. to let my husband shut down. This "Dr." Desai might argue that he offered the VA hospital option and that my late husband refused…well…wait before throwing the stone to Ash, "Dr." Desai!

Here is why my late husband refused to be transferred to ANY VA hospital:

Correspondence: Dec. 19th, 2006
To: Congressman John. M. McHugh
Adapted for: Aaron Garcia
Attorney Wrongful Death

I am trying to summarize below from my thirty-five (35) pages document about the Albany VA Medical Center. By the way, Ashley told me about the middle of November the 8th floor of the Albany VA Medical Center was under investigation - this is giving you an indication even if what we lived seems unbelievable, we really experienced it. Like there is an old French saying: "There is no smoke without fire".

I am totally and entirely sure Mr. Garcia the Albany VA Medical Center are the ones who trashed his liver and that's why the ammonia began to be totally out of control after a while at the Albany VA Medical Center.
There was a HUGE difference of his condition before going to this Albany VA Medical Center and after.

1- Ashley never had to take lactulose at home before his hospitalization at the Albany VA Medical Center;

2- He never had a high level of ammonia in his system at home;

3- He never said incoherent things before due to the ammonia going straight to his brain instead of being treated by his liver first. Never. (This is called encephalopathy - brain disease - caused by accumulation of excess of ammonia). To see a very intelligent man (even being a member of the prestigious Who's Who) in this state was heartbreaking to say the least but I understood quickly it was a temporary state;

4- Ashley went at the ICU with an ammonia level of 393 in a hepatic coma (at this point he could die) because the doctor who was supposed to check it did not. I observed during the afternoon and the evening the encephalopathy Ashley was experiencing – Dr. James County who was supposed to check his ammonia level told me in the afternoon that Ashley was "feeling fine". (and that's why I asked the help of the social worker Lori Bobersky right after) I asked repeatedly to James County to check his ammonia level on Veteran's day like he was supposed to do it in Saturday morning November 11th and I asked repeatedly to the nurse between 7:00 – 10:00 p.m. to take care of Ashley and she did not and unfortunately, Dr. Susan Rhee who was usually giving a good service (she was an exception) forgot to come when the nurse paged her at the nurse station twice – I requested it. (There are few good doctors and nurses but not enough to really do a difference at the Albany VA Medical Center) I asked Lori Bobersky to come see Ashley in the afternoon of Nov. 11th because he did something very unusual, to stick a piece of gum inside a new newspaper – I knew from that behavior the ammonia was going straight to his brain because he wasn't totally "himself" (because of the encephalopathy). Ashley replied to her he was tired and she "bought" that even if I told her I already saw many times Ashley tired and he never had an irrational behavior like this even with an extreme fatigue. Something had to be deadly wrong.... All Ashley was able to do is sit on his bed and to hold his head with his two hands bend his head and close his eyes – of course he wasn't able to ask for help in this state!!! The day after, another doctor called me at the Fisher House (located in the front of the Hospital) at 10:15 a.m. to tell me Ashley was at the ICU in the coma. At the ICU, Dr. Timofeev Stan was telling me that my husband didn't take his lactalose (he refused it but like I said he wasn't totally himself with all this ammonia going directly to his brain which is easily understandable) but he didn't know what happened on Saturday morning so I filled him in about the fact Dr. James County didn't check his ammonia level even if he was supposed to because Ashley had an ammonia peak on Thursday November 9th – the ammonia level was at 140 and because Dr. Susan Rhee heard me and used her head, she checked it and prescribed the lactulose so his ammonia level was at 100 after the treatment (the ammonia level of most people is about 20) but since he was at that point on Nov. 9th, they were supposed to check it on Saturday morning. If Ashley had known his ammonia level was high, he would be scared and would take his lactulose. One nurse at the ICU wanted to give Ashley Morphine (again !!!!!) when he had a Gastric Reflex. Even if I told her Ashley could surely have serious problems if he would take Morphine, she came back saying to Ash: "you are refusing to take Morphine" and I replied: "he is not refusing to take Morphine, he knows fully well he would have serious problems and most likely die" if he would take it, especially after this ammonia peak level at 393 and going to an hepatic coma. After 30 minutes of research for a painkiller because I wanted something better for Ash than Morphine they finally found the Fentanyl and that's why I know and found they could give him this painkiller when they did the "¾ inch tube procedure" but Ash suffered the Gastric Reflex for 30 minutes all right.

I am totally and entirely sure Mr. Garcia the Albany VA Medical Center are the ones who trashed his liver and that's why the ammonia began to be totally out of control after a while at the Albany VA Medical Center. Not before. That had never had been the case at home. (Anyway, the VA office in North Carolina and the VA Office of Massena is entirely responsible for not putting Ashley on a liver transplant list and even the Albany VA Medical Center were only considering the possibility of putting him on this list towards the end of his hospitalization - it is what they said to him and this is on records)

Here is why:

[1) Big surgery without a painkiller - a real torture. (the "¾ inch tube procedure") ¾ inch tube inserted in his body passing inside his belly, his lungs and finishing near his neck on Oct 19th, 2006 about 11:15 p.m. – not only that I know I truly can believe Ashley's words (he was an upright man) but also Dr. Ming Fey Luo told me and my husband had this intervention without a painkiller. They could at least find the Fentanyl if they would do their "homework". Of course, Ashley wanted to have this surgery because between the request for Ashley on Oct. 17th 2006 to go at the Albany Hospital (we were at the Massena Memorial Hospital through the VA office since the beginning of the day of Oct. 16th and the reason why he was finally sent by ambulance to Albany is because I pressured them after seeing they were letting Ashley suffocate - 2 times - with all this liquid in his lungs so I had more than enough) and also Ashley had to wait until Oct 19th about 11:15 p.m. to get this procedure done so for sure he was more than ready for this surgery and it's not something you should worry about when you are in a hospital if they would give you a painkiller during a big procedure…or not.

2) They offered to diminish his pain after the "surgery" without telling him they were about to give him Morphine. He trusted they knew what they were doing; but after the fifth shot he asked what they were giving him and they told him it was Morphine, which he did not want, but it was too late. Ashley's ammonia level went straight to the roof about 200 and was intoxicated for 4-5 hours, repeating "2-4-6" or "4-2-6" when asked any questions. It is all he was able to speak for hours.

I believe the combination of the two incidents mentioned above (1 + 2) put him in a situation he would surely be psychologically weaker and wouldn't think about the kind of help they were about to give him. (Morphine) (I have a Master degree in Psychology from Canada so I know about Psy stuff) Of course, he wanted a relief of his excruciating pain…who, with a right mind wouldn't want that?

3) The hospital fed him large quantities of proteins such as meat. Ash began to be yellow exactly on Nov. 26th, 2006, 4 days after the Albany VA Medical Center released him. His liver was worse than ever before.

(PARENTHESIS: I wanted so bad Ashley to have a liver transplant before his kidneys would totally shut down…but the last doctor in Massena Memorial Hospital, Nimesh Desai did not even offer a dialysis even if the dialysis center is part of MMH at just a couple of streets away on the main street. The woman at family services in the Massena Memorial Hospital (I don't have her name) offered us the possibility of a liver transplant from the The Strong Memorial Hospital but the reason why the offer was not appropriate (since the doctor told us Ashley had a maximum of 2 weeks to live and most likely only a week) she said that Ashley would have to wait at least 4-6 weeks to get it on November 29th, 2006 so from that point on, I began to write to the team of the Massena Memorial Hospital (the nurse told me that it will be on Ashley's chart so even Nimesh Desai will see it – he might have seen it but he certainly did not read those letters because he would see my determination) as well as sending him a copy of everything to the Congressman John M. McHugh by email and certified mail to his main offices because I was extremely stressed to see the kind of non-appropriate offer they were doing to Ashley and I even said to this "Pastor" Colin Lucid they were letting my husband shut down because I was seeing clear even if Mr. Desai was pretending to care and to crown the whole thing, "Dr." Desai tried the false guilt trip on that I was the one responsible for his sufferings. Mr. Garcia, I did the search about the fact a dialysis could be offered to prevent the kidneys to totally shut down as well as to prevent Ashley's death and to die this way was extremely painful because that is the first time I was seeing Ashley expressing in sounds what he was experiencing in his body and this totally broke me, that is emotional torture to see your husband dying this horrible way. In other words, the Albany VA Medical center trashed his liver and the Massena Memorial Hospital made sure his kidneys to shut down and Ash could die by suffocation at the Massena VA Office. A dialysis would most likely save my husband's life and I was willing to give a part of my liver to Ash because our blood was at least compatible (because I believe we had the same blood type – A+ but our blood was at least compatible) and this could be done to the Georgetown University Hospital and Congressman McHugh was fully informed of what this hospital could do because I sent him the information)

I don't wish to pretend to be a liver specialist (like them) but I believe the large amounts of proteins from meat did "the job".

Here is from a relevant source of information:

"This does not mean, however, that eating a diet containing enormous amounts of protein is the answer. In fact, it is unhealthy. Excess protein puts undue stress on the kidneys and the liver, which are faced with processing the waste products of protein metabolism. Nearly half of the amino acids in dietary protein are transformed into glucose by the liver and utilized to provide needed energy to the cells. This process results in a waste product, ammonia. Ammonia is toxic to the body, so the body protects itself by having the liver turn the ammonia into a much less toxic compound, urea, which is then carried through the bloodstream, filtered out by the kidneys, and excreted. As long as protein intake is not too great and the liver is working properly, ammonia is neutralized almost as soon as it is produced, so it does no harm. However, if there is too much ammonia for the liver to cope with—as a result of too much protein consumption, poor digestion, and /or a defect in liver function—toxic levels may accumulate. Strenuous exercise also tends to promote the accumulation of excess ammonia. This may put a person at risk for serious health problems, including encephalopathy (brain disease) or hepatic coma. Abnormally high levels of urea can also cause problems, including inflamed kidneys and back pain. Therefore, it is not the quantity but the quality of protein in the diet that is important (see DIET AND NUTRITION in Part One)".
Source:
http://www.vitamins-source.com/AminoAcids/

The Albany VA Medical Center put Ashley on a low protein diet (a sudden change of mind) at the end of his hospitalization when it was too late i.e. when his ammonia level in his body was just totally out of control.

In conclusion, my husband suffered a lot before dying and I am standing as long as I am alive to tell the truth about the way he died. In a letter to Christopher H. Lowery, VA Patient Advocate dated on Thu, 16 Nov 2006 21:43:29 -0500 (EST) I concluded this: "I am truly scared to leave to go back to Massena for just a couple of days to take care of what could ease Ashley's mind (and coming back to Albany right after) simply because of what happened. Most folks are dying before reaching a 393 ammonia level". (of course, I also wrote to the main doctor supervising the team around Ashley, Raymond Smith)]

At the time I communicated this to Aaron Garcia, I forgot to mention that Ashley learned he had the hepatitis C only two (2) months before his death and he learned that from the VA Office in Massena, NY before he re-entered for the "last round" in October 16th, 2006. (I will save you the fight I had to get a hospital bed for Ash because they were letting him suffocate twice (yes, 2 times) with all this liquid he had in his lungs) For the folks who know about the hepatitis C, you need to have the proper medication to stop this virus to literally "eat" your liver alive. So the blame goes to this "crappy" VA medical system who did not even deal with the hepatitis C.

..... but the Massena Dialysis center was at less than 2 miles from the Massena Memorial Hospital and Ashley needed a dialysis because his kidneys were shutting down and again, this option was not even offered to him. James Burnett was working in collaboration with Nimesh Desai and maybe under his supervision and he is the one who told me that Ashley will die and he surely did not care about my feelings at all because he did not offer the dialysis either and he could. At that particular moment, I was asking him to take a sample of my blood because compatible with Ash's in order to get part of my liver at the Georgetown University Hospital and he did not want to take a sample of my blood...because they ("Dr." Desai and "Dr." Burnett) intentionally mislead us to tell us he needed a liver transplant...well, not at the point Ash was...but he should see my determination to save Ash's life and should go ahead and offer the dialysis option...because now this is written in a book about to be sold because I got 124 hits in only few days.

I am 100% sure that Ashley would say yes to the dialysis.
Not only I have official documents attesting Ashley wanted to live but here's a poem he wrote about this:

Yes, it's True I Love my Life

Postmark: February 8th 2005

Yes, it's true I love my life
Even more I love my wife
I don't want to spend a day
With my wife so far away

Jut to see her loving smile
I would walk for many a mile
And she is my hearts desire
For she sets my love on fire

I have never had such love
As with her my soft sweet dove
She is so soft and so kind
I can't get her off my mind

One day soon you will see
My sweet Marie here with me
From my wife I feel such joy
I almost feel like a little boy

Ash

(Ash was type of person enduring/tolerating pain like a cat and I am now remembering very vividly Ashley moaning very loud because of shutting down for good (death) and I hear his complaints in my mind right now and it is very painful to me…He had to be in excruciating pain to moan like this because he had been beaten by his father when he was a kid like a dog several times because his father wanted to sexually abuse him and he was refusing so Ash learned to be tough….I need to have a conversation with the God of the Bible at the Cemetery in few minutes where Ash's body lies right after adding this to the text….Oh my Good Lord!…..I am sorry for the number of revisions of this book but please understand I am suffering yet because I did not see any justice done concerning what happened to us!) but my point is **that they criminally let my husband dehydrate to the bones** and I am avoiding since his death the image in my head because I could have a heart failure just to think about this! And this, I will never take it!

"Dr." Desai, you did let my husband dehydrate to the bones and he loved the life! How you could do such a thing???? May God send you right back to India to practice your war medicine in Jesus' name I pray, Amen! We already have enough of those criminally responsible doctors like Raymond Smith from the Albany VA Medical Center! We don't need you!

I did try to sue the VA hospitals but finally (yes, finally) an attorney was at the very least fair enough (we can not ask too much to those "liars", oups, I mean lawyers) to let me know the reason why they don't is because it's very expensive and very difficult so by the time I spin my wheels on the VA hospitals the Massena Memorial Hospital could get away with their crime to NOT offer the dialysis because you have so many months to sue and then, it's over.

Their leitmotiv in the US hospitals is, to put it plain, to let the poor die.

Like I said to Congressman McHugh on my letter
dated February 11th, 2007:

"I believe you care as a Congressman because you heard Ashley on May 24th, 2006 when I was in Montreal about this Visa business even if I wasn't heard by "Dr" Nimesh Desai. I wanted my husband alive. He could have a dialysis first - this was not even offered so is the dialysis center on main street in Massena, NY seems to be just for the rich people - and then get a part of my liver for a liver transplant second a.s.a.p., urgently. I wanted to give a part of my liver, I wanted to take the risks involved - I would be so happy to give a part of my liver to Ash. The dialysis was possible but this wasn't offered. Period".

Please ship Desai back to India to practice his **WAR MEDECINE**
and offer Smith to retire!!!!!

Well, I did not know from October 28th to December 5th, the problem was to get a dialysis a.s.a.p. because they gave us the false impression by offering to be on a liver transplant list that the liver was the problem but it was worse and they should tell us the truth but of course to tell the truth would empower us to save Ash's life and that is the last thing "Dr." Desai wanted. **Of course, if I would know at that time the solution i.e. the dialysis, they would have to kill me to stop me because I would disturb them until I would get it done if it was what Ash wanted and I am sure at 100% he would because he was very happy with me!** I do not trust the doctors anymore, period (in fact since the desecration of our marriage at the borders on Nov. 3rd, 2004 by the Canadian and the American border and Immigration guards, I came near of a heart failure about 12 times and I did not go to any hospital, I was dealing with God about the issue) and I have all the rights to not trust them because they did the Hippocratic/Hypocrite oath, which goes along with the Illuminati Mystery Babylon Religion anyway ...

I don't care what those allegedly specialists will tell you after the publication of this book. If they think that I got my masters degree in psychology in a cracker jack box, well they got theirs in the undiluted bull manure, especially those VA medical "doctors"! I know I have a good brain and I am using it and I know too well I am far from being hysteric, I am in fact very rationale.

You think I want their "damn" Swine Flu Mandatory Vaccine? You suffocate with it like you would drown. [they most likely will fine people of a certain amount of money per day or worse according to my researches – I hope I am wrong but it seems to go towards that hard line...You think I am afraid of death after all I went through with Canadian Immigration, US Immigration, VA hospitals, Massena Memorial Hospital, the US populace mentally abusing me while DHS playing with me like a cat killing its mouse until recently so I could not be functional most of the times, not even be able to open a bank account and drive my own car and finally Ashley's sister who did only give me 3677 dollars for the house? (please see the part titled: January 8th, 2005) Nope. Nothing will stop me to tell the truth and surely not the fear of death.]

Finally, here are the words of my friend, Adam Bartlett who knows me since 2001:

Letter of support wrote around March 26th, 2007

ADB4JESUS@aol.com wrote:

Marie,
I have attached my letter for you, send it to who ever is needed and make copies and send it to as many people as you think will help in this situation. God bless, Adam

----

Here's the letter:

Alpha & Omega

Outreach Ministries

P.O.Box 34 Boonville, Indiana 47601

Adam Bartlett: Cell:, email: adb4jesus@aol.com

Kevin Wilson: Cell:, email: kjw1975

Web Page: www.bibleheadquarters.org

To Whom It May Concern:

I have known Marie Buchanan for about 6-7 years and I also knew of her marriage to Mr. Ashley Buchanan. I also know of the ministry they shared and have participated in it with them on several occasions. I have followed Marie's battle with the American Government since her marriage and trying to get into the United States and gain citizenship. It is amazing to me how many "illegals" get the red carpet treatment yet a Veteran and his new bride are treated like communists.

The ordeal that Marie has had to endure throughout her marriage and Ashley's illness and subsequent death is something you would expect in a communist country. I am appalled at the way this situation has been handled and most especially the treatment in making Marie's transition into our country and literal nightmare.

I believe there should be a complete investigation into the V.A. Hospital that treated Ashley and I believe criminal charges should be filed against those that were negligent. As for the current situation about Marie's status into this country, that should not even be in question. This government owes it to the wife of a Veteran to make this situation right and stop harassing her in her attempt to become a citizen.

With treatment like this it is no surprise that there are hundreds of thousands of "illegals" because trying to do what is right is impossible with our incompetent government.

As an American citizen and a Veteran of our Armed Forces I am imploring you to do the right thing and stop this crazy charade with Marie.

Sincerely, Adam Bartlett

No Goats

Recorded: September 30th, 2004

Around our house we'll put two moats,
These will surely catch all goats.
In the moats we'll put some gators,
To munch the goats like tomaters.

Oh My Dear

Recorded: October 27th, 2004

Oh my dear what can I say,
I love you more each passing day.
I so long to be with you,
Share my love, this is true.

You mean more than anything,
You are worth my everything.
My special treasure from above,
My example of God's love.

I Love You,

Ashley

Only You

Modified: October 27th, 2004

Any time I'm feeling blue,
All I need is think of you,
All my troubles melt away,
And it is a brighter day.

Enchanting visions all so true,
Are the ones I have of you,
I so hope to see the day,
When I find you've come to stay.

If cold outside you know we'll huddle,
If inside we're sure to cuddle,
I wish each morn to wake and see,
That you're lying next to me.

Any time we're not together,
Regardless of the type of weather,
There's one thing you know I'll miss,
It's the taste of your sweet kiss.

And a thought I hold dear,
Is the one of you so near,
Be you dressed in jeans or lace,
I long to give you an embrace.

To gently wrap my arms around you,
And to say I'm glad I found you.
Another like you they'll never be,
And you mean so much to me.

Ash

Modified: March 21st, 2005

My proudest moment this you see,
Is the day you married me.
No prouder husband will you find,
Not black nor white nor any kind.

All my pride I have in you,
It's because you love me true.
A great treasure this is you,
Plus you're soft and pretty too.

I will always love you dear,
And I always want you near.
You are my love, you are my life,
And I am blessed you are my wife.

Ash

Sweet Marie

Modified: October 27th, 2004

When we're old and have gray hair,
Yes my dear, you'll find me there,
For I'll never run and hide,
You'll always find me by your side.

You'll always find within me love,
You are my gift from above,
The storms of life shall never part,
My sweet Marie from my heart.

With Love,

Ash

Tears of Pain Run Down my Face

Sent by email: March 29th, 2006

Tears of pain run down my face,
Not to find you in this place.
Many years I've spent in strife,
In a dismal empty life,

But now I have a loving wife,
That gives new meaning to my life.
Now every day I have no doubt,
That you, I cannot live without,

I plead my case unto the Lord,
And with it, I'm sure He's bored.
But He took my tears of pain,
Then He made me smile again.

Now He's filled me with His peace,
This separation's lost its lease.
Extended grief will be no more,
Soon we'll dance the number four.

Ash

Thank You

Modified: April 1st, 2005

Thank you for entering my life.
Thank you for being my wife.
Thank you for the things you say.
Thank you for your love each day.

I praise God each day for you,
For sending me a love that's true.
I'll tell you something else that's true,
I love you for being you.

I really wish I had you here,
I so long to hold you dear,
I really want to in this place,
Just to see your smiling face.

And when at last we are together,
Leave you dear, I would never.
When at last my face you see,
You'll know how much you mean to me.

Ash

The Days Go Past

As I watch the days go past,
I pray each one to be the last.
I can't wait to have you here,
For I so long to hold you near.

To hear your voice within our home,
I much prefer to the telephone.
I'd rather see you in our bed,
Than in the dreams within my head.

I'd wrap my arms around your hips,
Pull you close and kiss your lips.
Then I'll whisper in your ear,
"I'll love you more each passing year".

With all my love,

Ash

The Entrepreneur

Modified: August 9th, 2005

There once was a cat named Mr. Skip,
Who could catch a fly with his lips.
Now the way this cat made his cash,
Was not to dig in the trash.

For attention he'd act like a clown,
He'd get lots of folks gathered 'round,
Then reach down deep in his pockets,
Where he'd pull out Golden Lockets.

He made a good profit this cat,
His pockets were getting so fat.
With a smile he said "it isn't for me,
My owner needs a K3".

Ash

Thoughts of You

(Postmark: April, 2005)

Thoughts of you run through my mind,
And you know they're all so kind.
You are the one I love to touch.
You are the one I love so much.

I'd love to find you in my bed,
Not only here in my head.
When I think of love that's true,
All my thoughts turn to you.

I think of you all day long,
If I could I'd write a song,
Of a woman with eyes so blue,
Of the woman that loves me true.

Of the woman that married me,
Of the woman named Marie.
This lovely woman is my wife,
And to me she's brought new life.

Ash

Monday, September 27, 2004
9:45:18 PM EDT
Feeling Ecstatic
Hearing Angel by Sarah McLachlan
Marriage Proposal

Today I officially proposed marriage to a very dear woman named Marie Martine Hamel using this poem and she said yes making me the happiest man on planet Earth☺

She is the woman I have been searching for all my life. I had been praying and asking God for such a woman and He heard me. I had been talking to her for months before I realized she was the answer to my prayers. I thank God for her every day.

PROPOSAL

There are things I need to say,
I love you more each passing day.
Of all the things I could choose to do,
All I want is to be with you.

No more time spent all alone,
Just time together in our home.
For you are the greatest treasure,
I want us to be together.

There's still more I want to say,
I want you near me every day.
I want to end my single life,
And ask if you would be my wife.

I Love You Very Much,

Ashley

‘Twas the Night Before Immigration

Modified: April 24th, 2006

‘Twas the night before immigration and all through the house,
The cats danced number four, with Marie my dear spouse.
Her belongings all packed in boxes with care,
In hopes that help moving, soon would be there.

While here in Massena I was all filled with glee,
Knowing that soon, my dear wife I would see.
Now I have been dying to move her in soon,
For then we shall start, an endless Honeymoon.

Walk Across the Scorching Sands

Modified: June 22nd, 2005

Walk across the scorching sands,
Search throughout a thousand lands,
All these things I could do,
And never find another you.

I tried to find you on my own,
And always ended up alone.
Then I got down on my knees,
To ask the Lord, would He please,

Through His wisdom, by His grace,
To send me love in this place,
I longed for love in this life,
He sent me you, my precious wife.

Ash

Yes it's True

Modified: March 16th, 2005

Yes it's true that I love you,
And I know you love me too,
And I have a small confession,
It's that you are my obsession.

I often lay awake at night,
Wish I could just hold you tight.
On the day they made us part,
It tore a hole right through my heart.

One day soon I know we'll win,
Then I'll see your face again.
You're the one that makes me whole,
You share with me my very soul.

Ash

<u>YOU</u>

Modified: April 7th, 2005

If I could just hold your hand,
I think that it would be so grand.
I'd whisper softly in your ear,
And tell you that I love you dear.

I'd put my arms around your hips,
Pull you close and kiss your lips.
In only moments you would see,
Just how much you mean to me.

I'll come to you on each new day,
And you're sure to hear me say,
That my love for you stands true,
The only one for me is you.

Ash

APPENDIX

My Letter to my Congressman Concerning this Forced Vaccination

Dear Congressman John M. McHugh,

I did my own homework concerning this mandatory Swine Flu Vaccination (H1N1) and I do know they are able to force us because they forced me to take them before I crossed the US borders IF I wanted to see the face of my husband again. I loved him so much I decided to cheat on my health after those 19 months 1/2 of forced separation but my husband is dead now since Nimesh Desai did not even OFFER A DIALYSIS further to your phone call to the hospital officials on Dec. 2nd, 2006. The dialysis center was only at two miles from this "crappy" hospital, which in fact is not an hospital because they let my husband totally dehydrate by allowing his kidneys to shut down.

Here is one of the links I studied carefully:

THE FLU VACCINE RACKET

http://whale.to/vaccines/flu.html

Also, a conflict arises with me on those three levels:

A conflict arises because I believe that Man is made at God's image and the injection of toxic chemicals and form proteins into the blood stream is going against God's will to keep the temple Holy from impurities;

A conflict arises because I believe that I shall not mix the blood of man with the blood of animals. Many vaccines are produced of animal tissues;

A conflict arises because I believe that all life is sacred. The practice of abortion should not be encouraged. Vaccines are derived from aborted fetal tissues even though I do not have any other connections with the abortions of the vaccines that are derived.

Therefore, here is the ethical behavior I want to apply: as a Christian and widow of Reverend Ashley McDonald Buchanan, Doctor in Divinity and Honorably Discharged Vietnam Veteran, I think the life as a gift of God and the body a wonderful work of divine creation to be reverenced as the temple of God and I do not want this Swine Flu Vaccine to be forced upon me. 1 Cor. 3: 16; 1 Cor: 3: 6: 19; 1 Cor. 3: 17, 2 Cor. 7:1

There are so many things that were forced on me like this forced separation at the borders on Nov. 3rd, 2004 even if this was not only against the Constitution because we were a married couple but also was a desecration of our marriage, which was consecrated by nobody less than God the Creator Himself.

Even their own Immigration laws state this:

1) It's written this at: http://www.uscis.gov/files/form/I-130instr.pdf,

p. 4. : "When a petition is approved for the husband, wife, parent or unmarried minor child of a United States citizen, these persons are classified as immediate relatives. They do not have to wait for a visa number because immediate relatives are not subject to the immigrant visa limit".

Which means this border guard and this Immigration border agent at Ogdensburg Port of Entry intentionally did not even consider their own laws!

2) I had no return date to Canada on my Visa;

3) I even had 90 days to apply for an Immigrant Visa according to the Immigration laws, which was plenty enough to establish my credibility without being parted like vulgar cattle at the borders for 19 months ½! You need to remember that I not only had no criminal records but also a Masters degree in Psychology from Universite Laval, Quebec, Canada, including working experiences in various departments of the Canadian government.

They DESECRATED our marriage when God CONSECRATED us and this, I will always REMEMBER until my last breath! By the time I was reunited with my husband, another round was to begin this time with the VA "crappy" hospital system. Yes, the VA system is a very bad one:

http://www.kycbs.net/VA.htm
http://www.vamalpractice.info/

and Ash told me the 8th floor of the Albany VA medical center was under investigation when he was there from Oct. 19th, 2006 to Nov. 22nd, 2006.

Therefore, I certainly will not take more desecration from the authorities on powertrip, going as far as almost not allowing me to bury my own husband on December 11th, 2006. Without talking about our Christmas gift 2006 from US Immigration, which was to turn me back in Canada and the reason was this one: "they saw my face on t.v. and we were married! and therefore, I could not visit him, I had to wait the end of the Immigration process."

I am not only a Permanent Resident but also am an American according to God's word and God's word supercedes human laws but even as a Permanent Resident, the law protects me from that type of desecration.

My victimization and desecration is over in Jesus' name, the Jesus of the Bible, Mr. McHugh. In fact, I am more than sick of it. The US Constitution is protecting me as a Permanent Resident and therefore, I want to have a letter from you to show to the authorities when this forced vaccination will come to prove them that according to my Constitutional Rights, I do not want those vaccines and if they are so good, they just have to take "good care" of themselves with it and further have Alzheimer down the road because of this "crap" in their veins.

As a Permanent Resident of the United States, I want my health to be protected against this intrusion and desecration of the temple of the Holy Spirit, my body.

With Kind Regards,

Marie M. Buchanan

Give me Liberty or Give me Death! ~ Patrick Henry

Open Letter to Military Soldiers ~ Forced Swine Flu Vaccine

Important note:
Here is what the NWO did to my late husband who was
a Honorably Discharged Vietnam Veteran
born in Fort Dix, New Jersey
and served the US Navy

Many Internet people fear that the military will be used against citizens in regards to possibly forcing on them Swine flu vaccines, RFID tags, and internment in concentration camps. That would amount to war and crimes against the citizens. I have read that one of the direct effects of that vaccine is that it causes the lungs to fill up with fluid. The person died just hours after taking the recent version of the Swine flu vaccine.

Here is the **DESECRATION** , my dear late husband,
Reverend Ashley McDonald Buchanan, D.D., went through:

1) to separate him from his wife at the Militarized Northern borders on Nov. 3rd, 2004 for 19 months 1/2 - this was right at the midst of our honeymoon; thanks to DHS...

2) did not allow me to visit my husband for Christmas 2004;

3) to ask him to prove his US Citizenship when in fact he was born on a US base, which makes you automatically a US Citizen and also served the US Navy, which makes you automatically a US Citizen as well;

4) to force his wife to take the vaccines, otherwise she would not see his face again;

5) to damage his liver more with a high protein diet and to not give the proper medication for the hepatitis-C, which means the virus was literally "eating" his liver without considering the fact he was not on a liver transplant list yet;

6) to not even OFFER a dialysis at the last hospital he went even if I asked my Congressman to call the hospital officials, which he did but this action did not give any results, it was just another false hope for both of us;

7) to almost drop me in Canada like a piece of crap the day before Ash's burial on Dec. 11th, 2006 to be very precise, which almost prevented me to bury my own husband;

8) to not even tell me that I could bury him FOR FREE at the Arlington Cemetery - nobody told me, not even this pastor Colin Lucid who made sure I would be financially more in the hole (while DHS continuing to play with me) by meeting

this Funeral Home Director with me, who of course as the prototype business man, took advantage of the situation;

9) to want to make me pay 250$ when the NYS Whistleblower Paul Danko told me this could only cost 4$ to fix the military stone my husband is entitled to but the NYS Cemetery will not allow me to get MY military stone IF this ever would happen to stop the desecration I am under since Nov. 3r, 2004. All by myself with God, that's it. To this day, which means almost 3 years later, it is a pending project. Please understand this NWO broke me financially (I was doing 20$ an hour in Canada) and that is why I actually have teeth issues but Ashley was priceless to me and I have no regrets whatsoever that I shared what I had with him like he did with me.

Since "they" did that to my late husband, you are next if you are not stopping their very disgusting goal of population reduction. In short, the government does not give a "shit" (sorry for my "French" but that's the best way to put it) about you, my dear Military personnel. Deborah Reid's quote: "However, most likely the military leaders will not take that vaccine. They will get exemptions, but I doubt there will be exemptions for the lower level military soldiers".

More information at:
Open Letter to Military Soldiers-Forced Swine Flu Vaccine by Deborah Reid

Why be in a military that functions as an enemy to your fellow citizens, including your family, and yourself? It would be a smart idea to get out of such a military. You will find other ways to have your survival needs.

Very worthy suggestions at:
Open Letter to Military Soldiers-Forced Swine Flu Vaccine by Deborah Reid

It will be helpful to forward this open letter very much with hopes that it will reach all of the military soldiers and their families. Please forward even if this could cost my very life, (it might fall in the wrong hands) if at the very least my death could postpone this RFID/Mandatory Swine Flu Vaccine and everything related to it like the Concentration Camps, the Martial Law, then I would not die in vain and I would be this wonderful Immigrant like your own ancestors were, willing to die for her fellow Citizen.

A wounded "soldier" against the NWO,
In Loving Memory of Rev. Ashley McDonald Buchanan, D.D.
and for America
In the truth, I stand. (Jn. 14:6)

Marie Buchanan

Here is a representation of Ashley Greeting me in Heaven…

And here is a poem he wrote on January 27th, 2005
representing our life in Heaven…
he surely will greet me with a poem similar to this one…

<u>As We Walk Along the Way</u>

As we walk along the way,
Following God, the only way
On the bridges, over the steams
Towards our cottage of beautiful dreams

Around our cottage you will find
Beautiful flowers of every kind
Once inside you're sure to see
Cozy places for you and me

We listen to the small birds sing
As we sit in our double swing
You truly make this house a home
I'll never leave you all alone

Love,

Ash

and in his new poem, those thoughts below will be expressed:

"Oh My Dear Marie, I am so happy to see you again. The separation is over, Sugar and it's over forever. As you know God is good and He gave you a mansion next to mine. I am so happy to have you by my side…this time, we will be together

forever…having a perfect communion with God and with each other…you definitively are my preferred up here, you will always have this special place in my heart… Marie, the war against us is over, people will be rightfully judged according to their deeds by the Rightful Judge (it's written) so be assured they will not mess with us anymore☺
Welcome Home Marie!…."

My love of Ashley is strong as death (Song 8)
and Jesus is my Life
and I love the Truth, the Way and the Life (Jn. 14:1, 14:6)
more than my very life. (Ph. 1:21, Rev. 20:4)
http://www.andiesisle.com/inyouifoundme4dialup.html

Marie M. Buchanan, M.Ps.
For to me, Christ is my life and to die is gain.
(Ph. 1:21, Rev. 20:4)
http://www.the-truth-ministries.us
Researcher, Webmaster, Pastor-Assistant, Translator and Writer
Fighting for the truth online since December 2001
(20 links, including yahoo groups, blogs and videos)

Table of Contents

www.ingramcontent.com/pod-product-compliance
Ingram Content Group UK Ltd.
Pitfield, Milton Keynes, MK11 3LW, UK
UKHW051137260726
13967UKWH00010B/3102